Date: 9/19/17

J BIO MILLER
Gitlin, Marty,
Von Miller : football star /

BIGGEST NAMES IN SPORTS
VON MILLER
FOOTBALL STAR

by Marty Gitlin

FOCUS READERS

WWW.NORTHSTAREDITIONS.COM

Produced for North Star Editions by Red Line Editorial.

Photographs ©: Greg Trott/AP Images, cover, 1; Charlie Riedel/AP Images, 4–5; David J. Phillip/AP Images, 6, 22–23; Jack Dempsey/AP Images, 8, 25; Eric Gay/AP Images, 10–11; Mike Fuentes/AP Images, 13; Michael Conroy/AP Images, 15; Eric Bakke/AP Images, 16–17, 19, 27; David Zalubowski/AP Images, 20; Red Line Editorial, 29

ISBN
978-1-63517-043-6 (hardcover)
978-1-63517-099-3 (paperback)
978-1-63517-201-0 (ebook pdf)
978-1-63517-151-8 (hosted ebook)

Library of Congress Control Number: 2016951009

Printed in the United States of America
Mankato, MN
November, 2016

ABOUT THE AUTHOR

Marty Gitlin is a sportswriter and educational book author based in Cleveland, Ohio. He has had more than 100 books published, including dozens about famous athletes.

TABLE OF CONTENTS

CHAPTER 1

SUPER SUPER BOWL

The Denver Broncos were playing the Carolina Panthers in Super Bowl 50 on February 7, 2016. The game had just begun, but Von Miller was already dominating it. And the Denver linebacker was about to make a play that National Football League (NFL) fans would remember for years to come.

Von Miller (left) zeroes in on Cam Newton early in Super Bowl 50.

Newton is helpless as Miller chases his fumble.

Carolina quarterback Cam Newton took the **snap** from center. Miller flashed forward with amazing quickness. He raced toward the offensive line, cut left, and bolted around the end. Then he picked up speed and crashed into Newton.

A quarterback **sack** is usually a big play for the defense. But Miller took it a step further. He stripped the ball out of Newton's hands. It bounced into the end zone. Denver defensive tackle Malik Jackson fell on it for a Broncos touchdown. Midway through the first quarter, Denver led Carolina 10–0.

The Panthers fought back. With just under five minutes left in the game, they got the ball back on their own 24-yard line. They trailed 16–10. Newton had one last chance to lead his team down the field and score the game-winning touchdown.

Miller hoists the Lombardi Trophy at the Broncos' Super Bowl victory parade in Denver.

But Miller had other plans. On the third play of the drive, Newton went back to pass. As he tried to throw the ball, Miller knocked it out of his hand. Denver safety T. J. Ward recovered the fumble.

Soon the Broncos' offense scored the touchdown that sealed the victory. Miller's two forced fumbles had led directly to 15 of Denver's 24 points. He became one of the few defensive players in Super Bowl history to be named Most Valuable Player (MVP).

DANCING MAN

Miller likes to dance to celebrate sacks. But he did a different kind of dancing in the spring of 2016. He was picked to participate in the popular TV show *Dancing with the Stars*. His partner was professional dancer Witney Carson. Miller finished tied for seventh out of 12 celebrities on the show.

CHAPTER 2

HIDDEN TALENT

When he was growing up in DeSoto, Texas, a suburb of Dallas, Von Miller wanted to play football. But his father wanted Von to grow and get stronger first. He didn't think Von was ready to play such a physical sport. So when Von was in fifth grade, he plotted with his mother.

Von Miller intercepts a pass for Texas A&M against archrival Texas in 2010.

She drove him to practice and games. They kept his shoulder pads in the trunk of the car so his dad would not find out. Von changed into his uniform in the car.

When Von's dad learned the truth, he did not get angry. He was simply surprised that his wife and son had been able to keep it a secret for so long. He was glad his son had something in his life that he enjoyed so much.

Von did more than just enjoy football. He was great at it. But he also excelled off the field. His parents raised Von and his younger brother, Vins, to work hard and treat others with respect.

Miller developed into an elite pass rusher in college.

Von did not have great statistics at DeSoto High School. He managed only six sacks his senior year. He barely weighed 200 pounds (91 kg). College **scouts** thought Von was too small.

One scout who thought Von could play at the college level was Stan Eggen. He was a coach at Texas A&M University.

Eggen took a unique approach to **recruiting** Von. He wrote the young linebacker hundreds of letters. He wrote about playing with passion. He wrote about the impact Von could make at the school. He told Von he expected him to focus on education and earn his degree.

Only Eggen showed that level of interest. Von returned the favor by accepting a **scholarship** to Texas A&M in nearby College Station, Texas. Eggen would not be disappointed. Miller emerged as one of the finest college pass rushers ever. As a junior, he led the nation with 17 sacks.

Miller displays his skills at the 2011 NFL Scouting Combine.

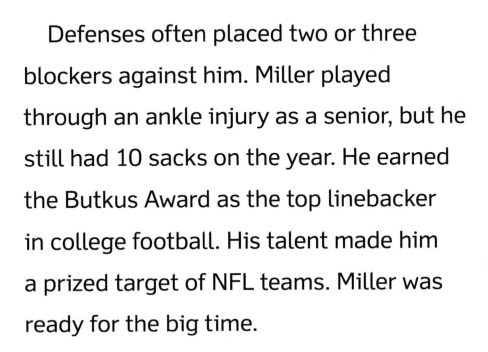

Defenses often placed two or three blockers against him. Miller played through an ankle injury as a senior, but he still had 10 sacks on the year. He earned the Butkus Award as the top linebacker in college football. His talent made him a prized target of NFL teams. Miller was ready for the big time.

CHAPTER 3

STAR IN THE MAKING

The Denver Broncos chose Von Miller with the second pick of the 2011 NFL **draft**. Some experts said it was a bad pick. They knew Miller could rush the passer. But they thought he would have a hard time stopping the big, bruising running backs he would face in the NFL.

Von Miller meets with Broncos legend John Elway after the draft.

Miller gave the Broncos what they were looking for—and then some. He posted 30 sacks in his first two seasons combined. He also used his quickness to cover receivers. And he improved his run defense.

Miller showed athletic skills that proved too much for blockers to handle. His rare combination of speed, quickness, and power soon made him one of the best linebackers in football. Offensive linemen marveled at how he could change direction so quickly. He beat them inside. He beat them outside. They simply could not keep up.

Miller sacks Packers quarterback Aaron Rodgers in 2011.

The ability to see clearly on the field was important to Miller. He had worn glasses most of his life, and he wanted to help kids with their vision as well. So in 2013, he launched a **foundation** called Von's Vision. It provides eye care for needy children.

Miller hands out glasses on Von's Vision Day in 2015.

The effort was a great success. In April 2014, approximately 160 kids from around Denver attended the first Von's Vision Day event. They received free eye exams. Miller was shocked to learn that more than 100 of them needed glasses.

He was thrilled to help them. He knew that good vision would help them in the classroom. He believed it would make their lives better. Miller had become a success in Denver, both on and off the field. But the best was yet to come.

A GOOD DECISION

Miller learned an important lesson in 2008. Texas A&M coach Mike Sherman suspended him that spring for missing study hall and classes. Miller threatened to transfer to another school. He was heading back home to DeSoto when his phone rang. It was his father, who ordered him to turn his truck around. He told his son that quitting was wrong. Miller was angry at first. But he went back to school and learned from the experience.

CHAPTER 4

NAVIGATING ROUGH WATERS

Suffering through bad times often allows people to better appreciate good times. And Von Miller endured some bad times. He had a miserable 2013. His trouble started when a dispute over a drug test led to a six-game suspension from the NFL.

Miller walks to the locker room after suffering a knee injury in a game at Houston in 2013.

Miller gained 15 pounds (6.8 kg) to help take on bigger blockers. But the added weight slowed him down.

Then Miller hurt his knee in December. His season was over. Miller could only watch as the Broncos were crushed by the Seattle Seahawks in the Super Bowl.

Miller learned from his mistakes. He went on a strict diet and workout program. He arrived at training camp in 2014 looking like his old self again.

He played like his old self, too. Miller recorded at least one sack in six straight games. He had nine sacks through seven games. Miller finished the 2014 season sixth in the NFL with 14 sacks. He was

Miller returned in 2014 in better shape and more determined to be an impact player on defense.

voted into the Pro Bowl for the third time in four years.

Miller wanted to be more than a good player. He wanted to be a leader on the team. He had been in the NFL for four seasons. His struggles in 2013 and comeback in 2014 made him believe he could help his teammates.

Miller continued to grow as a player in 2015. He put a lot of pressure on quarterbacks early that year. But they often unloaded the ball just before he could bring them down. He had only four sacks through the first eight games. But he piled up 12 sacks in Denver's next 11 games, including the playoffs.

Miller was ready when star quarterback Tom Brady and his New England Patriots arrived in Denver. A spot in the Super Bowl was on the line. And Miller made sure his Broncos got it. He **intercepted** a Brady pass in the second quarter. That led to a Denver touchdown. He sacked Brady twice in the third quarter. He added

Miller and the Broncos flattened Tom Brady and the Patriots in the 2015 playoffs.

five tackles. The Broncos won the game, and they were conference champions.

Soon they were Super Bowl champions. And it was made possible by the amazing play and leadership of Von Miller.

VON MILLER

- Height: 6 feet 3 inches (191 cm)
- Weight: 237 pounds (108 kg)
- Birth date: March 26, 1989
- Birthplace: DeSoto, Texas
- High school: DeSoto High School
- College: Texas A&M, College Station, Texas (2007–2011)
- NFL team: Denver Broncos (2011–)
- Major awards: 2011 NFL Defensive Rookie of the Year; 2016 Super Bowl MVP

Denver

DeSoto

College Station

FOCUS ON
VON MILLER

Write your answers on a separate piece of paper.

1. Write a sentence that describes the key ideas of Chapter 4.

2. Do you think Von Miller's mother should have told his father about Von playing football as a child? Why or why not?

3. How many sacks did Von Miller have in his first two NFL seasons?

   A. 24
   B. 30
   C. 33

4. Why did the Broncos draft Miller in the first round in 2011?

   A. Their coach liked players from Texas A&M.
   B. They needed to improve their pass rush.
   C. Their owner liked Miller's glasses.

Answer key on page 32.

GLOSSARY

draft
A system that allows teams to acquire new players coming into a league.

foundation
An organization that is created and supported with money that people give in order to do something that helps society.

intercepted
Caught a pass intended for an opponent.

recruiting
Persuading a high school player to attend a college, usually to play sports.

sack
A tackle of the quarterback behind the line of scrimmage before he can pass the ball.

scholarship
Money given to a student to pay for education expenses.

scouts
People whose jobs involve looking for talented young players.

snap
The start of each play, when the center hikes the ball between his legs to a player behind him.

TO LEARN MORE

BOOKS

Ellenport, Craig. *The Super Bowl: More Than a Game.* Broomall, PA: Mason Crest, 2016.

Gigliotti, Jim. *The Pro Football Draft.* Broomall, PA: Mason Crest, 2017.

Rogers, Andy. *Who's Who of Pro Football: A Guide to the Game's Greatest Players.* North Mankato, MN: Capstone Press, 2016.

NOTE TO EDUCATORS

Visit **www.focusreaders.com** to find lesson plans, activities, links, and other resources related to this title.

INDEX

Answer Key: **1.** Answers will vary; **2.** Answers will vary; **3.** B; **4.** B